By Astrolabes & Constellations

Agave Press Manuscript & Portfolio series

By Astrolabes & Constellations
Text copyright © 2019 by Cristina Querrer

Agave Press Manuscript & Portfolio Series
ISSN 2641-9963
Editor: Ariana Lyriotakis
All rights reserved.

First published in 2019 by Agave Press.
Portland, Oregon USA
http://www.agavepress.com

Book design by Grant Macdonald

Without limiting the rights under copyright reserved above, no part of this publication may be used or reproduced in any manner whatsoever without written permission except in the case of brief quotations embodied in critical articles and reviews. Your support of the author's rights is appreciated.

ISBN: 978-0-578-47795-4

Printed and bound in the United States of America.

Table of Contents

14	There is No Vocabulary
15	From a Retired Disco Queen
16	Mango Man
18	Bruises
19	My Daughter, Where Will You Go?
20	To Begin Again
21	What Would Frida Kahlo Do?
23	Itch
24	Japanese Woman in Micronesia
25	Lover, Tell Me War Stories
26	Island in the Clouds
27	Form an I
28	Homeless

29	Goodbye, Paradise
30	Gestalt's Chair
31	At Low Tide
32	Poet in Seven Days
35	Blow Out the Lantern
36	My Republic
37	To My Conquistador
38	Delicacy
39	At the Outpatient Pharmacy
41	Dragonfly Wings
42	Reconstituted Tango
43	Night in Niantic
44	Breadfruit & Taro Chant
45	Intensa Mirada
46	Theory of Hands

47	Life without Sugar
48	Today, Lolita
49	Tears of Things
50	My Time Traveler
51	Rugged Diction
52	Ritornello Principle
53	Espiritu
55	Unideal Daughter
56	My Ill Attempt
57	Three-Mile Run
59	Pockets
60	There is No Leaving
62	Ako
63	Subsequent Sorrows
64	Before I Forget

65	My Barrio by the Sea
67	The Lava Experiment
68	Second Language
70	The Manila Envelope
71	Muted Abyss
72	Dear Sylvia
74	King of Pentacles
75	My Mother's Rosary
76	Papaya Tree Prophecies
78	Broken Map
80	Maelstrom
81	Propositioning the Orbit
82	The Anomaly of Physics
83	Vitriol
84	Underwater

85	Off the Grid
86	Composition of Air
87	Orchid Grower
88	Death March
90	Aguirre Springs, NM
91	Atlas of My Days
93	Scarecrow Girl
94	Martial Law
95	Cognizant
97	Acknowledgments
98	About the Author

PREFACE

When I think of creative pieces that captivate and enthrall, I am most taken by the ones that invite us on a journey, both literally and figuratively. Whether illuminating words or art, these are narratives of time and place that fill our senses with the beautiful and the intimate, the tragic and the uplifting. These works allow us to reach beyond the limits of our everyday, to engage not solely with the discernable expressions of life, but also with ideas and thoughts that push the realm of our collective experiences.

As we opened our search for writers and artists to highlight in this series, Cristina Querrer's *By Astrolabes & Constellations* emerged as an exceptional emblem of the meandering path, an aspect of storytelling we esteem so highly. Having grown up in the Phillipines, her youth defined as a U.S. military child moving from place to place, she has imbued her work with a sense of migration and wayfaring. This publication, her first full-length poetry volume, brings together questions of self, identity, travel, nostalgia, loss, and forgiveness, and examines what it is to be the product of circumstance.

We are pleased to bring this collection to press as the debut work in the Agave Press Manuscript & Portfolio series.

Ariana Lyriotakis
Editor

*Built a paper boat;
it blew away
to far off lands—
drifted back
& anchored itself
back onto this island…*

There is No Vocabulary

Sit awhile until the light dims,
and I can no longer read the words.
I read your spine like Braille instead,
and tell you your story.

How many times does the summer
have to leave for your return?
Perhaps as many times I turn the pages
of this never-ending story.

There is no vocabulary for us to rely on
just precarious verbs
like leave/stay and leave again.

Are we imitating the ebb and flow,
the depression, the swells?
Where in nature does it love?
Through the creation of creatures like us,
perhaps, scurrying about blindly
in the abundant sand.

At some point someone
should say, "Enough."
We have listened long enough,
lived through the denouements,
digested every little moment:

epic crescendo of a lover's laughter,
lilt of a sigh upon the bough,
an afternoon's weight during heartbreak—
losses collecting in catchments and eddies.

From a Retired Disco Queen

My waters, thought to be haunted,
turned away many expeditions
but you discovered southwest passages,
guiding your independent craft,
your astrolabes and constellations
to the strobe-lighted platform where I danced.

There are many lives that were made of this,
just like my poor mother who endured
such cessation of sound that I could not stand
the stillness of her womb, where my penchant
for crashing endings came into being.

Neither are you a victim to all of this.
You, the circumnavigator of truth
dictating your life to the exactitude of a compass,
charting sunrises by military standards
while I openly study the behavior of birds.

Fatherless conversations, attracted to subterfuges,
I am an orphan in my own right—
impassive Amerasian girl at the nail salon,
a detached disco queen at the go-go bar.

No equal transaction because I dance for you
and you never fill my heart's deep pockets.
I have unloaded my past residences upon you.
You crassly offer me a sparse word.

I amble off the dance floor.

Mango Man

I.

I remember the vendor
who pushed his squeaky cart of sweet corn,
sugarcane, and mangos
in the sweltering afternoons,
through residential subdivisions of my past.

As a child I chased him down,
with my only peso in hand,
anxious to fulfill that nameless need
in my early dawn. It's just as if the sky
turned the colors of burnt orange
and the world smelled of incense
and my grandmother's coconut oil,
I walked this path before
with many faces of my past.

I returned here with the same perplexities—
gastric questions that bubble inside,
back pains of my former loss.
My mother will one day look on smiling,
finally, at rest in her hammock
contented for once about the heat,
as I will hear again that mango man
calling out the objects of my affection.

One day pockets will overflow with pesos
and I will never rummage through
that garbage pile of pits—memory.
Just as if the Bataan Death March of my life
took me down cramped corridors
separating me from my husk.

II.

I am still eased here by
visions of water buffaloes and rice paddies,
fish set out to dry in the tangerine sun,
and the store owner sleeping
with the fly swatter in his hand.

Something unexplainable ferments,
something in my sultry past falls short,
and far beyond my torturous
initiation to salaciousness.

Yes, my first lover experienced me here.
A foreigner himself. Many more
that could not fulfill that nameless need:
the permanency, the offer
of an endless ocean brimming with
sea life, a depth of ancient knowing.

I never left these prostitute alleys—
the shadows of naked silhouettes haunt me:
the scurry and hustle of the night scenes
in this sex capital of the world
still clamor in my ear.

I became a part of melding masses
of ants crawling into the crevices
of the cabarets, of go-go girls and GIs,
San Miguel beer and rotting mango seeds
littering the dirt floor beneath their feet.

Bruises

It is the watermark
in the middle of your paper,
stained and buckled,
no amount of straightening
can bring it back
to its original form.

It is usually visible:
a rusty coffee stain
perpetually serves
as a reminder of the mistake
you made
placing your coffee cup
on a piece of paper
that is now valuable.

More insidiously
it is a thunder cloud
staining the sky
with the blackest of all ink,
permanent as the day
without relief.

It causes unwanted creases
on your slacks,
pulls out all your hems,
and leaves more
than your paper in disarray
because no one feels them
but you.

My Daughter, Where Will You Go?

Like walking effigies
easily dismantled

bodies of paint-by-numbers,
so easily constructed

perpetually suspended myths
that never tell about itself

that never know where
the center of the storm is

My daughter, where will you go into the night,
when many days go like this?

I offer you my words,
your great-grandmother's ghost

Go into it carefully as if it is a dark forest
like the mouth of the jungle

I had no one to say to me that is
not me in her

or

that is her in me

that we should hold hands
and not be strangers

As if we were born like this
for a reason

To talk a language of forgiveness
to the suicides

To Begin Again

No heavy furniture to weigh on me now,
just a million tangled hangers
and piles of paper push me
to throw away all forgotten things:

old receipts, plane tickets,
dire poems, an old picture of an ex-lover
uncovered in between them—
I never pause, don't blink an eye—
never knew who I was then.

A younger woman smiling at the camera
with my beau, whose name I barely remember,
lifting my glass, toasting life. I don't care
for filled rooms anymore,
even forgotten how to stay up at night.

I only care now that my next hefty courage
comes in the sound of my voice,
the shape of this room,
with me in it, reading, transfiguring,
imprinting myself into these new battlements.
Amazing my body still moves, though, still dances,
remembers all the complex steps.

What Would Frida Kahlo Do?

She wouldn't try
to pluck her eyebrows
to please you
she'd celebrate it
she'd paint it
even emphasize
that third eye

She'd paint a crime scene
of her husband
cutting her up with scissors
unos cuantos piquetitos
in response to him having sex
with her own sister

She'd move far away to France
& paint the gory scenes
a million times over
her twin with the same heart
they came from all over to see

She'd cut her hair
& dress like a man despite him
I bet she went to the witch doctor
& conjured up spells

& Diego didn't even know it
because he knew well enough
he fucked up
& would stay at her bedside
till the end

In light of all this
I will place a needle
in the poppet
in place of all the pain
& write your name
in those blank spaces
& chant at midnight

I'd write this poem for relief
so that the world could see
what I ever saw
in someone who
didn't even paint
write poems
start a revolution
or even gave me credit

Frida, well, she'd just
laugh at you
& flick her cigarette

Itch

The turn of events—many of them—
turn up on my face now

Each day, a step further away
from a former self,
a shell, skin I have shed.

Things are falling apart now,
hinges on door frames squeak,
rust found in most inauspicious places.
One day I woke up and got
a frozen shoulder, and my skin itched so much
I just wanted to skin it

Everyone—people I have loved—
become strangers, yet I am loved by relatives
I have never met

Each passing winter,
but especially this past winter, was hellish
looking at succulent fruit
that flaunt their vibrant skin & how warmth
always included them

Color has left me—sometimes, though,
it appears briefly like a flitting hummingbird
and I am running like a child again
down Plaridel subdivision just happy to be playing
The order of the day plays itself out
without anybody noticing

One day explanations go out the window
and must be satisfied
being categorized and filed away
silently in the night

Japanese Woman in Micronesia

In her late 60s, she still walks from the heart of Nett all the way to Kolonia. She gave birth to five sons here. Three of them own the only restaurant that made noodles from scratch. One of her sons married a young French woman from the northwest region of France whose eyes did not match each other, one light blue and the other, hazel.

Sharing a taxi into town, crammed with other strangers who listened on, we talked of how I came here, and how it all came to be, but mostly of her long list of long-time associations, like a teacher from the college long ago who played flute while she sang and played the accordion.

"Say hello to Chen for me and to the other Taiwanese instructor," she turned her head to me as she passed the dollar to the taxi driver and in seemingly fluent Pohnpeian, shared pleasantries with him. She then slinked out of the cab in her curtsy-like manner, as I watched her walk away in her flat strap-on sandals with socks, her colorful Micronesian lava-lava, and bright yellow t-shirt.

Lover, Tell Me War Stories

Correspondences to my youth that never wrote back to me:
the lack, the leverage,
the luscious landscape of vim and vigor.

Withhold meat of memory. Close your eyes,
and sink your teeth into my thigh! There is no wilt
in my laughter, no sag in my lusting.

Lover, tell me war stories: all the prostitutes,
all the Madonnas, but never baring your breast;
the smell of control is still on your collar.

We, prisoners of war—a treasure trove of poverty,
deficient, delinquent, defunct, wish to break free
from these inane exhibits you would gladly pay for.

Island in the Clouds
for Pohnpei

If Gulliver trounced up these peaks
He would find that he could scoop the sky
Into his palms —but the gods built these
Invisible bridges for those who brave the heights.
Below, the people trudge through arterial woes
Heavy and burdened with bulky ballasts on their backs,
Heaving with reddened smiles between the sweat.
Their unleashed dogs yawn and laze about the asphalt,
Their children walk to school alone on
Narrow roads where cars hazardously drive by.
Mothers take infants and toddlers to their hips —
Go up and down these hills with no hurry, and the fathers, well,
They walk through these paths with machetes, drenched
In last night's sakau and full of betel nut spit.
Gulliver might say too primitive yet will stay
To laze around too—for his wife, from the outlying
Islands, would have settled here for the elevation and the rain
That sweeps and feeds the canopy well, although good nutrition
Will be scant—as distant and rare as American dreams.

Form an I

handouts of Anton Chekhov
and Flannery O'Connor fill my folder

awaiting a youth far-removed from
literary lives
literary devices

uncommon as nuclear families
low gas prices
and unripened tomatoes from afar

I teach O'Connor's
literature of poverty
the irony of Chekhov

in attempts to connect
pot-hole-ridden roads
to their village
weeding through texts
of familiar Pacific voices
at night trying to meet them
by the waterfalls

surely there is one to
start to form poetry
to say what she never could
to conquer colonialism
a forced god

to weed-whack a new path
up a mountain where she

had never seen
she will now
know what it means

to mark an *X* and form an *I*

Homeless

The borderlines
have moved in my heart—
the casted line has been pulled
way underneath
to unfathomable depths that
I cannot trace my roots anymore.

I thought that was the only way
I would know who I am.
What if I followed that line
all the way back, all the way under?
I'd never come back—
and no one would know.

I am what I once was:
single-celled protozoa
roaming the darkness
picking out specks of plankton
groping for flashing, sparkling light.

Goodbye, Paradise

Cargo boats dotted the harbor
and at this height on Sokehs Ridge,
I knew I was in the middle of nowhere.
So, I ran all the way to the end
of the causeway where the island
falls off to the jagged reef
of abandoned boats and carriers

where the only airline picks up
dead weight on certain days.
The pink and blue georgette floral curtains
still flap during gusts of wind,
I'm sure of it.

And on certain days, the tuna boats
come to dry the ocean out
dredging the bottom of its soul
retrieving the bulk of its heart.

You cast your reel out on those days
by the freshly sunken industrial tuna boat
returning home by sundown to those
Micronesian floral curtains,
with fish caught in deep waters—

living daily with no solidity,
strolling home drunk again,
chasing mermaids in the dark
with no deference,
no me to guide you to safety.

Gestalt's Chair

A single chair is love over time;
it becomes the thing of the past—
present-centered, Spring's tree—
assured & promising.

But when uncared for
memory of ax & nails
ache at the limbs
& weakens the legs.

It paints itself a self-portrait
eulogizing your agony.
The earth narrows to this corner
& what was once seen with clarity
becomes senile & bedridden.

Soul over body,
adoration over repulsion,
glee over grief.
Everything connects,
everything inferred,
straight-backed—
solemn, imprecise form
in the dimness.

At Low Tide

Words are but pebbles in the mouths of these men.
Perfunctory, perhaps—groping common gestures of virility.
At the stoop, they gurgle evening greetings like salt water.
The women watch, encroached, silent,
breath withheld, wink-less—forever astonished
by the language the men possess. They live with them,
grew up in the same huts—yet side by side apologies
never spool off the tongue, discontentment
never rolls off the back— rum, cigarette stains
and blood from late night brawls washed off
by morning. Even young boys speak it
like broken English. In the back room of the nipa hut,
baritone voices bond with the shadows
of a flickering candle flame by their perpetual discord and only while
making love do the tides fall—
this moment when one can walk
so far off shore into the ocean, all the way
to the nape of a woman's dream with nets
that still come up empty.

Poet in Seven Days

1

It comes in blues,
dark and deep with melancholy.
Tones low and monotonous.
I cannot think above the clouds.
I cannot think about flowers.
I cannot think past 9 p.m.
So, I sleep and slink
into my forgetfulness shedding
all this nonsense of lasting,
for I am of no use to anyone.

2

It's no better looking into
my coffee for a clue—swirling
cream of clandestine charm—
Come hither! Reveal thyself!
The laundry summons me,
my child heckles at my chase and work
grunts at my priority, *poetry*?
This poem stuffed in my pockets
with pieces of me and miscellany,
proof of my lowly vocation and residence.

3

Pages numbered, ordered, perfect.
I sleep with the lights on this time;
I rise a little earlier —alter the way
I live and love by the philosopher of the day.
Shred all my old bills, discard irrelevancies.
Even open my desk for a lovely criminal
to sell me illicit descriptions of shadows.
My dog looks up in disbelief,
moans and stretches as the clock ticks louder.

4

Relinquish asking my coffee for answers.
Surrender asking questions at all.
In my next life, I will have no children,
I will come back a man, never apologizing
and abandoning every chance I get —
'tis the perfect stock for poetry!
Forgive me for these passages,
as I forgive those who never
wanted to know—

5

That there is splendor the way dishes
are stacked uniformly and my clothes
folded just so, in planning a future
by college Lit courses—
my shoddy attempt at status quo.
To be degreed and dignified!
There are daycare costs and my car note.
But out of all my debtors,
my biggest expense are my dues to poetry?
For Lorca sips tea in my living room!
Elegance exists at last!

6

Next on the grocery list, cereal and milk.
Perhaps Marianne Moore can give me
tips on dating? Gwendolyn Brooks can
school me on no-good men.
What if Frank O'Hara was my uncle—
what life I'd have then! Here comes a good one,
oh, where's my goddamn pen?
I curse and blunder for
it lies in the abyss of my purse.

7

There now, wait!
My child asleep in my arms,
her breath in unison with mine—
no words, no theories,
no redolent sign. The day collects
like residue on the furniture—*You feel it?*
I asked her earlier—*the wind?*
She in delight of it closes her eyes
with her mouth wide open tries to swallow air—
snippets I put away in my wallet.
Not enough, I know—
but every year's mishap restores itself right here.

Blow Out the Lantern

The rain came down so brutally,
it washed away my island.
What is there to leave for you now?
No strength of mind,
the body sodden with memories,
cannot row the boat to shore anymore.

Weather pattern's gone awry—
the arctic cold veered into the tropics.
No medicine, no inoculations
to prevent this disease from settling.
Oh, frightful rocks pounding my body.

Was once so spry. Was once so fearless.
Found a cave beneath the waterfalls,
now my body lost to the wild.
The wind finally blew out the lantern.
Didn't get a chance to mark
this spot on my map.

My Republic

My language is not yours
I was born brown
Into an unknown tribe
Subterranean, native, cave dwelling

My body is not yours
It's turned into something frightful
Bent over and arthritic
Stretched-marked by the weight of you
Not young, sweet,
Oriental beauty you're used to

My country is not yours
Anarchy built this
Not corruption, not religion,
No caste system—only governed by
A woman who knows her body
Like the terrain of this island
And the many faces of identity
Under any God-forsaken rock

To My Conquistador

I needed intensity: the verve, the gash, my proclivity for pronouns, of persons still weighted by persistent years of wavering. Oh, sweet seneschal, my Seneca snakeroot, terms of requisite allowances. Only wisp of smoke wafting through cracks and crevices; you are but a thousand turned backs, postulating artificialities, preoccupying my inner sanctum. Go now.

Give me seclusion far from collision theories, ye wreckers of respite, ye unbending expression, just a curious crate of cowards crowding my mind-style. Law of constancy forbade resistance to you, but I must. Oh, how I must! The moment when I first heard footsteps, my tribe was stirred. Decoded the Chocolate Hills of Bohol, my colossal combination, broken.

Gargantuan god-head, you stole my sacred rice mat, sucked the red, betel leave juice of my veins. You now go into the stars with your atlases, just reconcile me, please, only to precipices and countenances of clouds.

Delicacy

It's easier to mask sunlight
with dark curtains
while The Great Wall of China
goes on for miles and miles.
But this sensuous sentinel
opens her gates at night
while you ride away
with her spiritual livelihood,
just to feel the breeze on her body,
a disparagement to her cause.

It may seem nothing can dispirit her,
but she is a mere emblem
that embodies men
of stature and courage
who want nothing
of lasting legacies,
like cities they plunder.

They dismember her slowly
by their fear of flowers.
She, but a statue of indulgence,
a place to discard their brokenness,
a delicacy for heroes and cowards.

At the Outpatient Pharmacy
(VA Hospital, Bay Pines, FL)

In hospital robes, encumbered, embittered men
mutter irritably to the nation, each pushing himself
in his wheelchair by his only leg.

Scuttling through the hospital halls two of them
nearly collide at the Continental Divide
between the lobby and the exit door.

I watch it from the other end of the hall
as I wait for my prescription,
constantly looking down at my blue slip,
impatient for my Last Name, First
to come up on the digital board.

As minutes pass, I wade through
the sea of old men, the woman part
of this wild civilization of souls,
detached by conformity,
misled knights fed by the King's propaganda.

I always longed to be Joan of Arc,
but only a few years in the Army
earned me this right
to be waiting next to radiomen,
cooks, and bombardiers.

Female commanders upstairs
get their yearly breast exams.
A nurse is educated on a different PTSD:
she was raped by the desk sergeant in '79
walking alone to her barracks at night.

We all pay a price for the honor,
measured by Purple Hearts and Honorable Discharges.
Injustices remain like puss in our wounds.

There is no drug the interns can administer
to the hearts of the broken tin men and GI Janes.

I sit with these men having conversations
about Agent Orange and conspiracy theories
from a war I was made from, *Vietnam*.
Fathered and left behind by a GI
as another GI took his place.

I still talk to my fathers
wondering why I became a casualty here
where war lives on even when
the sun shines every day.

Dragonfly Wings

You bring me the paper every morning.
We talk about the weather
and what's on sale,
talk about the latest trivialities.

Conversations are filled with them.
The streets bend and swerve
and tilt with uselessness.

I drive on them every day—
I drive by broken buildings,
trash heaps of insignificance.

But I want to talk about war,
and how I was born from it,
and how we can never stop fighting.

Yet I wait for my parcel from afar—
a package from my twin sister:
a torn sari, a lock of hair,
a piece of flesh taken
from her from a disgruntled lover.

And I will send back a letter
with a feather, dragonfly wings—
remedies for a broken bone,
a gorged-out heart.

I will reveal to her maps of the internal—
topography not found in this travesty
among empty bowls and broken shells,
or a knife, a gun, or words that chained.

I was and am still like her
cowering in the corner of the hut.
And I keep telling you every day
I am waiting to hear from her.

Reconstituted Tango

Embryonic, this prefix to love.
Feeds off embolic whim and fancy.
Exceedingly exosmic,
this slow state of waning.

Silent upheavals overturning
this governing body like a foolish,
young rebel among the hills,
raw with pure insight,
a predisposed blindness.

I glide on the bright red lipstick,
always too overwhelming
for my shade. I apply it again,
and again, and again.

Such subjugation!
Constantly wearing that beet-red,
bloody dagger and hollowed skull
behind the mask! It cannot be helped:
forever caught between half-steps
and rudimentary lessons.

The dance: second nature.

Night in Niantic

one stippled moment
crammed into dreams

a far east morning
exotic living-room table book
all about wild orchids

yet we ignore downcast jungles
during new england nuances

of salty air   and ella fitzgerald

of a mild and quenchable riesling
of sultry selections

glasses tipped

strips of bark strewn
and mornings after ghosts walk over
niantic bridge

walk right by sad shapes
still longing for something
to save them from

these reckless evenings   these reckless
raspy blues singers
of wanting more wine
in this niantic fog

Breadfruit & Taro Chant

A little piece of breadfruit
A little piece of taro
A little piece of reef fish
A little piece of marrow from
A little piece of dog

Sail away with me to Chuuk
Sail away with me to Kosrae
On an outrigger beyond the reef
Where the swells will devour us

A little piece of tuna
A little piece of marlin
A little piece of martyr
On the way to heaven

Intensa Mirada

(to all the Pablos)

Poco a poco, one by one
the fleet within your iris
orchestrates the ocean

Take each form to a new level
organic/industrial

Each innocent broken bird
beneath your canvas
is a deadly venture for your muse
for she would
lose everything

Otherwise you would be soul-less—
& how could you go on to fuel yourself?

Dead bodies since your death
but you left us such art!

Blood: their blood
in another narrative
another scene

How men would love to be you
but they are no different

Digest them through your eyes
in return for your magic

Theory of Hands

I have written all my life in the palms of hands.

And those that intentionally closed
to suffocate my well-thought-out words,
not one has come generously,
confident, with a firm repose.

The intentions of fingers
are like misguided charity,
a philanthropist who never sat with a beggar.
I have left behind a poem for each knuckle
to soften the jagged bones of a fist.

Yet, they were used to oppress
the sissy-poet who lived on less
to write about afterbirth,
a bruised eye, a comrade, dejected times.

I have learned to replace hands
with a forearm or a wrist instead,
to pull me up when my knees gave out,
or when my heart caved in.

If there is anything I memorized,
it would be the contours of each hand
that pried open my hold.

Life without Sugar

Imagine hard bent days without saviors.
The world headed by arithmomancy.
A world without Neruda's neologisms,
his *leaning into the afternoons*
and his talking about *sweetness, always*.
Imagine not tasting
the granulated grievances of the gods—
gluttony becomes too much,
despair becomes decorous.
What would we be doing
staring into the sugar bowl?
What right would we have?
Delectable the days can be
without processed predicates,
oily fascinations of casual observers.
We are blind not to savor
pure sunrises from the interstate.
Real chronicles are in cookie jars,
gourmet wrapped fancies
flower in your orchard.
Bestow honeycombed catacombs,
vestiges of casabas and star apples,
all-encompassing succulence
surrounds you now:
to be blessed like this.

Today, Lolita

She's a critical citizen—
arranges & nests her nihilism
into colorful flower pots

Derrida nods knowingly
at her attempt for order
despite her only attracting
middle-aged used car salesmen

You know the type:
Typical skewed picture
in a crooked picture frame
insisting to stay cock-eyed forever
despite her wanting the design of
straight, clean teeth

Comes in and messes with her laundry
hanging on the clothes line
Laughs incessantly,
& screws with her many minds

Today, she's Lolita, tomorrow, Sylvia,
martyred Penelope of yesterday

Waiting for a man,
a deconstruction, thereof,
O, mangy dogs that come
to eat her heart out

But if she can lose weight,
she will be young again,
& she can have her
wherewithal with whomever

Yes, today, Lolita—yes, girl,
he can't tell you nothing

Tears of Things

   Truth is,
tears are what I know so well.
Infestation of tulip poplars
infect the eyes, attenuates,
then evaporates. Little beasts
in the foam stay,
abeyant to seasons.
It lies dormant until all fruit
have been eaten.
These steadfast friends to sorrow,
are well-kept, well-fed.
Made their permanent home
in the cellar of my skin,
in the bell tower of my thoughts,
stream of possessed dancers
in the night is all
I hear and see.

My Time Traveler

~for Uncle Ben

the whole world moves
marching and mourning
beyond safe perimeters

a filipino marine: my uncle—
died in manila
shot: 1970s mindanao
fighting guerrilla forces

young body dappled with medals
displayed in the casket

in the middle of
my grandmother's nipa hut
in the middle of
the mottled afternoon light
when two other marines
stood at attention by his side

the world moved in jolts and fits
had curious geometries and sounds
was too young to know
how light connects with shadows

how combat boots
paced the bamboo floor
for many years to come
my mother tells me
he still visits us from leave—
he's hiding behind the couch, she said
hiding from the enemy—

the war smolders on

Rugged Diction

He said at his age, "My Dearest"
and concluding a letter with "Love,"
strikes a deep chord of meaning
that should not be taken lightly.

But what he meant was
it should not be taken lightly
by my lower class of wisdom—
my age that would never care
to delve nor decode it.

Plus, he said "dearest is a superlative,"
meaning, I suppose, that it must
proceed with a pronoun, someone's name,
particularly his, probably in cursive writing,
or italicized or bolded with elegant fonts.

But what he does not know is
how I am being more concerned
with the texture of paper,
curious about the rain in Seattle,
knew what it meant when he said
he felt like "a ludicrous Toulouse Lautrec."

Ritornello Principle
~Typhoon Haiyan, November 2013

I saw the body form here
on the weather radar online,
when Pohnpei, Micronesia,
was being pummeled by rain.

It was when the storm passed us
did the radar show
a small swirl that unbeknownst to us

would form into that evil eye
that would devour Yap,
the trail of tiny islands,
and then my people.

A super storm—off the charts—
people in the Philippines
with no way to defend themselves.
Helpless was I as the news unfolded:
Australian news, BBC, CNN Asia,
and the Filipino channel report
of death tolls rising.

Small, treeless, strips of land,
falling off to the sea,
overcrowded and naked.

I pray the government
move them to higher ground in time
as I sing a tragic aria for the suffering
and pray for light and relief
as the theater curtains
open and closes again

in a once familiar scene.

Espiritu

Rub that tiger balm on aching dreams.
Light the mosquito repellent at night
and surround your bed
with the mosquito net,
which cannot protect you
from those people of the past.

When one dies, they say,
dead names can never be spoken,
for the jealous spirits
shall dance in the delight
for things of the living,
even for the matchbox

that sat on your nightstand,
just in case you woke up at night
during one of those city brownouts
and you needed a light
to see your way out
of your childhood.

And the Haitian man you once loved
shared his spirit stories with you
under the ceiling fan.
You wonder if he made you love him
by his legitimate magic.
For his island recipes
are now mixed in—
not far removed from yours.
He knows of papaya and passion fruit,
as well as you do.

Though when others see—
they see dark and light,
no common strand
which is visible to the eye.
If I die now,
I tell you not to keep my hair,
but my poetry.

You may speak my name
every now-and-then,
so I may play with the matchbox
or the venetian blinds while you sleep.

If you hear me, you will know I have loved you.

Unideal Daughter

Yes, I ran away
to get away from people
I thought I knew
to the arms of strangers
that could have raped me
killed me

Yes, I ran away from a home
that didn't feel like one

plastic curtains
plastic covered couches
ashtrays overflowing
with cigarette butts
a cabinet full of liquor

Yes, I ran away
to drink and smoke in bars
to dance like those women
you like to watch

Yes, I ran away
to only return to a mother
who made her life
for a father—and is bitter,
very bitter

My Ill Attempt

Every day,
I honestly don't know
where I'm going.
Tedious routines
recur like evil spirits.

I try to etch out poems
and my bulky narratives
in between crammed spaces
constantly filled with disorder
and I am constantly
sifting water out
to keep my paper dry.

It is my ill attempt
to preserve all what my life was,
for it was something
even for just a fraction—
even when one lover became another,
even when my country became another

      — amid all these wars.

Three-Mile Run

Slough off misconceptions
of what might be,
roll on the deodorant,
tie up the hair and those battered shoes.
Forget makeup.

The Army taught me
how to cowgirl up,
defend and kill if need be
by someone's command,
survive gas chambers
and night fire, while my babies
were back home sleeping.

More than ever now, the importance
of softness, the ripeness of
thick thighs are what moves me.

For muscles are mechanical,
unsympathetic music.
But it's been three days
since I took my run.

At Fort Jackson, my biggest fear
was rappelling off that 40-foot wall.
Once I did, I told drill sergeant
I'd do it again.

I ran golf courses,
survived good ole Tank Hill,
held highest PT scores
during boot camp graduation at 27.
Now, my one-mile marker
is the barber shop on St. Pete Drive,
or is it Jack Willies just down a piece?

Two-mile marker is the middle of
Route 580, somewhere, ending on that street
I always forget the name
that runs right by my place.

I think of a lover, my youth,
and who the hell was it
that turned me on to sangria?
Each wretched step,
a prayer for my relatives
I cannot save from poverty
and a query:

Why didn't I re-up in the Army
if it made me so tough?
I suppose I could do an extra mile,
but I won't

despite young boys in Mustangs
that honk at me on the road,
or even the broken neck old geezers
in pickup trucks.

I laugh. Do they know I've aged,
am divorced with children?
That my chance in getting hit
by their car is far greater
than finding love?

I measure life this way:
How much discomfort I can endure.
For I may never walk again
or drive umpteen miles
to just talk to you for a while.

Pockets

But there are pockets more permanent
where things are kept,
things that were handed to you: a piece
of sugarcane fresh from the market,
grandfather's handkerchief,
tender messages on the back of matchbooks.

But there are pockets more invisible
where you keep things too,
such as the constancy of tides,
elapsed sketches of reverie—above all, love—
at the center of time.

There is No Leaving
to Gabriel García Márquez

I wrote my farewell letter also
many times, in my life,
on grains of sand, on various shores.
I still have nothing
to give to conventions.
I am just a woman who has given up
on romance.

Every night, lately,
I return to empty tables and chairs,
even my pots and pans seek attention.
On my back porch,
my crimson geranium
lost its life due to lack of affection.
Many dawdling deaths.
But you remind us we have been given
an inestimable world,
the bravado of a baby's breath,
insurmountable seas.

You also reminded me
of my Filipino grandfather, *Amang,*
as I last saw him,
eroded by toiling a lifetime over an ocean,
trodden brown body and beaten hat
on a small fishing boat that once bore my name.
You made me remember him
and how much he must have loved me
though we spoke different languages.

Tonight, you joined me at my table,
kept me company,
read me love letters from life,
lead me back to the center with roses.
I promise to embrace more, to know
that my romance is happening now.
But you see, I live in a house of memories
of all those who left me behind. In my house,
there simply will be no leaving
if I have any say so at all.

Ako

Ako[1], I started as a dissident somewhere between
two long planks of phraseologies languishing between lost prosaic.

Ako, I unearthed my bones in deserts, in tundras,
in islands, wherever I migrated as a meandering misbeliever.

Ako, then I began to sing songs from my barangay[2],
embedded music most familiar like fetal murmurs.

Ako, then I began to tend to my flowerbeds
most meticulously, weeding out rain forests of lost time.

Ako, then I learned to sleep soundly
even when sudden surges overcame my terrain.

Ako, I woke up to wakefulness, wonder and incredulity.
The seas feel me, the sky sees me. They always have.

1. I, me (Tagalog) 2. Village, town, subdivision

Subsequent Sorrows

Just in time to relieve one
from too much smiling.
Then it comes in sequence,
feverishly, making its own erratic cycles.
For some, it is a bizarre inundation
of nails and pitchforks.
This universal tourist takes pictures of your tears
then shows them in highbrow galleries,
turning your musk into wine.
Tears, it says, *such harrowing beauty*,
tilts its head and laughs.

Before I Forget

Just in case the leaves turn color,
before my words unfold the awful truth
of how a bitter fruit was once
sweet in our mouths while exchanging
deserts for fertile forests,
algebraic equations for no absolutions.

Just in case the world turns
against us, or was it ever there
for us? Yes, indeed I say—
it was always there— all-encompassing
joys and sorrows that crowd our hearts
so much that we could not prepare
for chances, we vacillate
in between set measures.

Just in case I lost interest—
will I ever? But in case I lose
my sight, my hearing,
or all my mobility,
jot it down, right here, right now—
that we were here in earth's bed,
mellifluent, silvery twines, embracing.

My Barrio by the Sea

I held my mother in my arms
when she relayed the sad news
about my aunt.
This is how she held me
when I was a child.

I felt the currents
of Legaspi Sea pull us to shore.
This is what happens when
your memory outweighs you.
If I were born another time, another place,
I would have known sadness just the same.
But its permanent residence
is in that nipa hut by the sea.

Reciting polio and hunger—
a baby cousin who died at two,
small body unornamented,
the women knelt in black
and a humid night listening to
concerned voices stirring
in the next house, through
the morning ocean air
and the squeaky communal water pump.
Then came the sudden wail—
an undetected storm.

This has always outweighed me.
My mother has not seen her sister
since we left the Philippines years ago,
now she is ill—I hear
my younger cousins having children—
I wonder if they suffer from atrophy
of the consciousness as I do
when I hear occasional news
of births and deaths—
tucked away behind
thick tapestries of distance.

Home is no other shores, planets,
future galaxies, and not even
the time and place of your birth.
It is letters from your youth—
summers at the barrio, trips to mountains,
and the smiling, barefooted,
naked-bottomed children in the sun.

How lucky I am to have these
and be tormented
by the warm hand on my neck.

The Lava Experiment

I.
You burned my eyes and scorched my brows,
inched on, your mouth agape, devoured
the Spanish churches of my past.
I stayed with you as long as I could.
Heard your belly groan and you wanted,
plainly wanted, for mysterious need.
You turned without warning. I ignored the signs.
At the very least, did not evacuate
the women and children.
I wanted to go on thinking that we could coexist.
But I cannot sleep with tigers.

II.
Those nights when you were still,
I watched the rise and fall of your chest,
many a civilization. Nothing new.
And each time you took in a breath
you drew me closer and closer.
I stopped watching the clock,
heard the church bell ring,
the dogs stopped barking, and then
the unenviable release charged through my window.
You climbed on my bed and burned my lungs
as I lay with clenched fist. A pointless protest.
But this is what no scholar cares to explain.
Ah, but look at you!

III.
I have studied your movement as a composer would,
battling every cantata, reliving every repertoire.
You tried to hold back your nature.
This is where I know, more than any place
I have lived, my petrified form beneath the ashes
in between your deep, black breaths.
Someone will one day predict your eruptions.
One day, someone will touch me
the way you did without killing all the trees.

Second Language
~to Neruda

But for the experience,
I will purchase shells
that I can pick myself for far less,
to gladly have you guide me into shops
to touch the textures of your canvas,
your fabrics, barter with you for your smile.

You have unknowingly woven yourself
in and out of me. Taken aback
by your sudden outburst in libraries
or in quiet halls, I feel at times at lost
in your ulterior fringes. I am wanting
the calyx of your throat
describe to me your oceans,
your terrain of meanings,
hoping to live in translation.

Verbalize in your language,
in your tonality, express to me
what it means in your country
to engulf a wonder, suddenly with no time
to digest it fully.

But the sweet taste of it
will forever linger on your palette
and shall fiercely crave it again
so that you would risk your life
to cross the Rio Grande
from suppressed verbs,
or on a crowded vessel
on top of musty bodies
floating fearlessly to autonomy.

Right now,
I tell you what it means in mine:

It means my heart yearns
to be elliptical as the planet in orb,
suspended by the myths of allegiances.
Though, where I live is not
without aberration or without
spurious dictator that seeks
to damper my escape,
but I found equanimity
in other words,
I could not find within mine.

The Manila Envelope

A mud-stained envelope trampled
and threadbare on the ground
reminds me of *Manila*,
the city in my birth country,
I've visited long ago.

Malformed bodies of beggars—
pendulous stumps and bare feet
wounded virgin pages
with crude etchings.

All the while, merchant ships
sailed along the coast. Even way before
discovery of flight lived stories, songs, travails—
like seedlings stuck to
tender tendrils that germinate the lover —
Empress who will never be exalted.

Reach for it and jostle for appellation—
for these soggy poems within it—
leavening words sodden with seawater,
aged as yesterday's yeast.
Whomever receives this massy missive,
save the damned, save the poor.

Muted Abyss

How does a drowning girl
reconcile herself to the notion of air?
Will it keep her alive?
Perhaps purity is an illusion
that stops her from surfacing.

Finally, a line is thrown in
from the same man
who pushed her into the water.
A saintly silhouette, looking down,
wanting unconditional love
while she's gasping,
writhing in the muted abyss.

Yes, she saw others
as hopeful fathers towing the same line.
She hung on until it tired her out.

All it takes is pulling her in as if you mean it.
If she stays below too long
she will become the rusted anchor
without a line.

The search party,
in their diving suits now,
hope to recover the lost medallions.
There's a seahorse swimming
between all the treasures.

Dear Sylvia

I wish to hear from you from those depths.
Are things clearer there now?
I know dolphins speak to you.

I wish you could tell me your secrets
within the wells of your words.
Does the Gestapo still haunt you
on the other side?

They still live, I can assure you.
I seek to hoard the maps.
Hide the escape routes
in my satchel. Leave trails
for those who care.

They say they do.
But they don't care to find me.
My feet are dangling.
The birds circle above
and I speak to you below.
Oh, my Lady Lazarus.
Lady of the Lake.

Have you found Camelot?
Are you still yanked by little smiling hooks?
Memory? Do you have them?

It's what cannot be erased here.
Weights on ankles.
Inconsiderate people.
The world is full of them.
Dolphins click in my ears.
Angelic messengers.

Must I hold on so tight?
For whatever for?
Sleep on it,
on little travel pillows,
travel light.
Be light, soundless, weightless.
Don't move too fast. Don't feel a thing.
For you will drown again
by people you left behind, Sylvia.

King of Pentacles

You talked about heady nights
and sailing to your Conch Republic
with an epicurean delight for solitude and stars.
Anyone can be taught to sail, you say;
indeed, I nodded on the other side of the phone
as I pictured you, a lone star cowboy
corralling in his horses for the evening.

Walked in one day wanting to do yoga;
we exchanged trinkets and things,
and that was the extent of it, really.
Sitting in your well-engineered fortress,
no cares, been on your own too long,
can't remember how to follow through
with courtesies, for anyone else's formalities.

I understood the magnetic poles shifting part,
and sprinkling whiskey overboard to the four winds,
another earthly man who loves the sea,
but I am but a seafarer myself
just collecting exotic shells of stories
into my jars to watch them glow
and burn out like fireflies.

My Mother's Rosary

O, how I long to be your porcelain Madonna
on the corner of your altar adorned with candles,
ancestral prayers and offerings.
Maybe you'd take notice the girl
you took to Sunday mass,
who couldn't wait to go to the cathedral
to see its grand courtyards
aligned with carts of prayer books and rosaries,
see the man who sold rice cakes and sampaguitas.
I watched you every Sunday
whisper prayers under your breath.
I watched your fingers every Sunday
glide over those smooth beads.
I longed to be them for the warmth
of your kneading, the missing pertinence.
But it was a ritual like yours, I grew
not to notice, or at least I thought.
Televised mass would suffice
on this side now as you become more unfamiliar.
I came to tell you I can't go with you anymore
as a girl stuck to your side, still longing
to be held regularly as your rosary.
I now kiss my children's faces
reminding them I am far from holy,
many miles from the altar,
far from relentless faith of old women.
I wonder what I will become.
And they, too?
Will they see things move under veils?
Hear church statues talk?

Papaya Tree Prophecies

an island shaped like a heart I wore
unnoticed on my silver chain
holding in my throat
an old language
of myths and legends of greenness
of every young guava

the sun burned yellow-mango,
over-ripened, oversized fruit
on the stem of a girl

it was said the man
that owned our house
had buried his treasures
in our backyard
under the papaya tree
before he died

I fed the invisible man
when I was five every day
with food from the table
in return for his lavish tales
that froze me
to that concrete courtyard

One midnight
my cousin woke up
in a cold sweat exclaiming
that if my family did not leave
the house he would
take me with him,

and sure enough,
I had a fever so high—
like an apparition,
passed everyone unsuspectingly
with food from that night's leftovers
still in my pocket
They woke me up
that one equatorial summer

but I walked out with you anyway
this past winter into the

Atlantic

Broken Map

I continued this broken map
on paper napkins
on back of my bill's envelope

sticky notes
my breasts
my eyelids

for fear of it veering off
for fear of falling off
& I would have no trace
& no moment
to go back to & say
that's where out there
in the Pacific
at such and such time
the boat turned over
& the couple drowned

sometimes it's best
to let the sunken ships lie
be forgotten
let the scuba divers
pick through its ribs for gold

it was a shame
the captain was greedy
he wanted more
young coconut meat
& endless tuna

& back at shore
I kept stitching the sails
kept the coordinates up
like cadence

though impossible now
to get back to anywhere
let alone know where
it began & why

Maelstrom

and won't ever recall
the frozen faces of my Adonis

the reason for our beginnings
shoving into each other

like a restive crop of seaweed
emotive to spontaneous action

rumors of this sinking ship
the irony of grandeur

what do I owe to the cadavers
the skeletal remains of broken-hearted

cast-ironed soldiers,
foul-mouthed machismo foretelling me?

imitate the unchanging calm of sunset
they say cast afternoon's net to sea

scatter yourself out like frantic schools of fish
but consider cloud formations because

the difference in this ever-variant world
is as steadfast and furious as storms

no matter if I remember—just memory
of mania, *opus de mi maestro*

of obsidian, mother of pearl—
whirling irregular surfaces and upsurge of debris

Propositioning the Orbit

The cure is an anecdote
from someone's forgotten life—
faded tickets from
our favorite concerts
now used as bookmarks.

A cigar in the study,
leather and mahogany
moist with memory,

someone reading about someone
on the other side of you
converging on a bamboo raft.

History has positioned itself to you
and the correctness
of the compass has followed.

It followed me to the sea cliff,
to the promontory of you—
for oyster divers have faith
and permeable in respect
to our geometry.

Remember scars of comets
that marred this landscape
of instance.

The Anomaly of Physics

What fills this place
with old weapons
are longitudes and latitudes
of a time and place,
prevailing marks
that never leaves us.

On the clothesline of balance,
stars could be taken by negligence
or by distorted glances
at the mural of the deceased.
But the telescope points skyward,
into bedrooms, offices, alleyways.

As we get closer,
sharpness is dulled.
Spend all our lives calculating.

One turn of a misaligned planet,
a contorted moon,
makes us unable to move beyond
a fixed position
where we annihilate ourselves
and abandon our lovers.

Lucid gowns pulled over sullen cities
establishes the contentment
of basis in fact:
laws of gravity become
null and void to the dying
and naked infants, pure.

Vitriol

the rumbling begins after a star-filled night —
sometimes scarcity of words
follows lava from an angry volcano

singes the foliage,
burns down the house yet flowers thrive
in these conditions, somehow

escaping lava flow, the brazen ash
isn't worth their existence anymore

& stopped returning to the abandoned hillside
where no one comes to live

but volcanoes do not care
they cannot help themselves

& will do it again & again
until it claims all the space

pushing out the greenery
pushing out the color

fooling the next civilization
to build a world around it

to do it all again

Underwater

Like the old restaurant that was built
on Tondaligan Beach so long ago,
its whole trunk suffused,
forever lodged, frozen like
Medusa's victim as the tide rose and fell,
the waves beat on its body time and time again—
proof of slow, painful decay.

I lived through my own revolutions and anarchy.
I am bent toward an unknown direction,
my crumbling faith with underwater caves,
adjacent to shipwrecks.

Imagine that restaurant in its heyday, overflowing
with customers and laughter
and the leaning coconut tree down the shore—
wonder when the last time it stood erect—
a strapping tree, wrenching its neck,
as the children climbed on it?

Off the Grid

Skirt the usual derelicts who linger
at the surface like water spiders
skimming the plane, frantically claiming
their little leaf on the water.

Circumvent useless situations—
morning commutes to misery—
homeless mystics maddening
at the bough of afternoon rush hours.

Be home with softness, lush space
of salient symmetry, smells and sounds
of earlier days.

Be the commanding conductor of your backyard—
hold shavings of wisdom among synoptic garble
cluttering the air waves. Go back to immeasurable eras
catching tadpoles after the rain.

Hear the fullness of life in your chest—
the pop and sizzle of your synapses
when the symphony composes itself before you.

Welcome it all between your toes—
what we once knew so well. Love fractals, prisms,
dandelions. Turn on nature's surround sound,
see through its own high definition screen—
not society's cacophony that obstructs this view.

Unplug yourself from it.
Decipher the Sanskrit and discover crop circles.
Read the *Riverside Anthology* by candlelight.

Composition of Air

It exasperates me
If I can just know
Where it's coming from
I would know the source
The reason for its existence
But then it ends abruptly
That silence itself is more persistent
That I forget about music
About what reasons for sharing
For breathing in summer dearth
That I long for shelter deep in the thickets
Of things, far from humanity
Because I want to hide myself
Because no one will care
If the Winter Solstice
Or the Mayan calendar
Were keeping the right time
That they predicted perfect alignments
Of stars, foresaw futures
I know music even exists in all
Vacuous spaces & somber universes
That they exist because of it, even if
The ear can't find it, even
When you can't change the channel
And turn off poetry,
You can't deny its distinct hum

Orchid Grower
~for Kuya Ling

It is so tempting in the barrage
of uncertainties to grab the scalpel
and dissect the heart,
each overture, the intractable light,
the blind side that can take you out.

I cannot inure this to form,
though it takes the shape of sleep,
has wings of a monarch butterfly
and is fixed like memory's coral reef.

As much as I fought through jungles
to search for the language of the gods,
deep in the thickets are waterfalls,
that yellow fever, scurvy
and panic-ridden farragoes
can never deny me.

Be that assiduous belief that propels me
to the apogee of Mount Arayat
that once stood at the foothold of my youth.
I scurry between jeepneys,
like a vein's transport from life's
checkpoint to checkpoint
and like the legend of the mermaid
that earned her legs,
I walk through the city markets
under your yellow umbrella.

One cannot dissect the wild orchid
to learn how to perform miracles.

Death March

*In anticipation of the annual Bataan Memorial Death March,
White Sands Missile Range, New Mexico, April 1999*

In the chaos, I left all my belongings.
I have lost many addresses,
phone numbers,
in my series of disconnects.
These hyper-variables existed
as long as I have.

They wonder where I am,
if I decided to do it.
In the chaos, I have been told
to give up all that has
ever sustained me:
excess baggage,
a water retentive heart
that sagged so long
with the weight of others.

Yet I speak of useful utensils.
I speak with my mother's tongue
that was taken away from me
when I was five.
Now my words rise above
the traffic of world news
and float with other prayers
to the nucleus of the sun.

I have dug up my bones
to drag myself here
half across this earth,
marching for lost souls in jungles.

I have scraped
the bottom of the ocean floor
marching 26.2 miles in the desert
donning a 35-pound rucksack,
full army gear, canteens,
with all our lives on my back.

Aguirre Springs, NM

The day on the desert mountainside
and on that black licorice night,
I felt like Picasso's women
with fragmented bellies and breasts.

So, there was the one spot—
the pulse of creation, the womb,
the heart you by instinct touched
with a boy's wonderment.

The thought still pricks me
like insouciant cacti
how we met at the stream
very dry and thirsty.

Atlas of My Days

I. *Morning of Madness*

There is no glow,
No song, nor summer
But grief
In this silent fissure
Where nothing grows.
No seasons return
To color the leaves.

But leaves,
They fall —they fall
Till movement no more
Makes one get up
Time after time
To the joys, distilled.

II. *Daylight, Drab*

Father of duty
Haunts the days—enslaving
The feeble.
Salivating dogs respond
To curdling blood
Rising to the surface.
They fight, still fight
In killing fields
Of each country,
Of each century —
Concomitant cries

For provisions.
Spirits, dispersed.
Wings clipped.
You would think
It was nightfall.

III. *Earnest Evening*

It is worse to want
The mornings
To come faster
Between life's breath:
Birth and death —
The reason, none.
To lie awake

While others lie clueless
To unforeseeable years.
Love, overturned
To unreturned giving
In slow, squalid successions.
Going now,
Sleep, give way.

Scarecrow Girl

To stand herewith, spanned-like,
soaking up the rain
and yesterday's dirt dripping
from my toes,
joining other muddy trails.

I, all follow with
no inkling of immensity,
just a dashed line—
where someone will
come barreling in
eventually without forethought,
screeching into these silent fields
I stand watch.

Here, there is a parody
to a universal sense of balance,
at least from what
the black foragers
from the sky show me.
Therefore, I continue to stand,
barely, feeble in my attempt
to look like a woman
in an iron dress.

No need to feed me
dignity through spoons,
because I am beyond
the growls of necessities.

Happy? Yes, quite happy
being a scarecrow girl
with straw guts.

I am also so proud, so proud,
because I can stand so still,
spanned-like, after even knowing
I will never be resurrected.

Martial Law

Trapeze artists know not
of one good solid stance
one pure motionless act

To levitate in one spot
from one residence to the next
leaving behind forever a strand of hair,
a shoe— heck, even my whole
damn heart

To find oneself again and again,
but never taking root—
Necessitate the distance
between your mother & mine

If only I knew where
the same back streets
& alleyways are again

I'd remember the sirens,
the dictator's curfew,
so that I may take hold

finally climb
the barbed-wire border wall
& collect all
the shards of me

Cognizant

Lovers come, firm in spring,
then unsure when winter comes as usual—
children, demands, what now
of romance and me,
my strange solstices
and requests for time?

Sometimes this bungalow
shudders at my isolation,
yawns at my dull routine,
toothbrushes stand
like little sentries in the jar.

I pace the wooden floors,
pray to ceiling fans,
stare and stare and stare
into the offing.

Then I read about you
and want to go, too,
where there is ample time to write,
to fall back into the sea,
to climb santol trees like I used to.

But listen:

The cantaloupes are on sale,
and so is the cereal
that my children love,
and my handsome date
is bearing flowers
at the moment

...all I need to know for now.

Acknowledgments

Field of Mirrors: An Anthology of Philippine American Writers | PAWA, Inc.
"Ako," "There is No Leaving," "Before I Forget," "Tears of Things," "Life without Sugar," and "Poet in Seven Days"

The Art of Exporting | dancing girl press
"My Mother's Rosary," "Papaya Tree Prophecies," "Propositioning the
Orbit," "Underwater," "Off the Grid," "Composition of Air," "The Anomaly of Physics," and "My Time Traveler"

Literary Juice Magazine | "Breadfruit & Taro Chant"

Literary Well | Carayan Press
"Aguirre Springs, NM," "Rugged Diction," and "Theory of Hands"

The Fairfield Review | "Mango Man" and "Espiritu"

With Gratitude

Thanks to my family and friends for their steadfast support, particularly to the artists and writers who have supported my work and continue to be an inspiration to me such as Eileen R. Tabios, Luisa A. Igloria, Nick Carbó, Bino A. Realuyo, Frank Montesonti, and Ira Sukrungruang, to name a few. And thanks to my friends and former colleagues at Pohnpei, Federated States of Micronesia, who have influenced some of my Pohnpei poems. Of course, many thanks to Agave Press for giving me the opportunity to present my first full-length poetry collection to the world.

About the Author

Cristina Querrer was born in the Philippines and grew up as a U.S. Air Force military child. Querrer is also a U.S. Army veteran and has earned her MFA from National University. Having been raised in the Philippines, Querrer also lived in Connecticut for many years before moving to Tampa Bay, Florida where she continues to write and to create. This is her first, full-length poetry collection.

www.ingramcontent.com/pod-product-compliance
Lightning Source LLC
Chambersburg PA
CBHW021020090426
42738CB00007B/847